Hi Everyone,

Thank you so much for purchasing this Jade Summer book!

We have a surprise for you...

This book includes a **free digital copy** (PDF format) so you can print your favorite images and color them an unlimited number of times.

Make sure to visit our website to preview our other books, view completed coloring pages from fans, and follow the Jade Summer brand on social media.

JadeSummer.com

Yours Truly,

The Team at Jade Summer

P.S. Do you know someone who would enjoy this book? Buy them a copy and make it a surprise gift. We promise they'll love it!

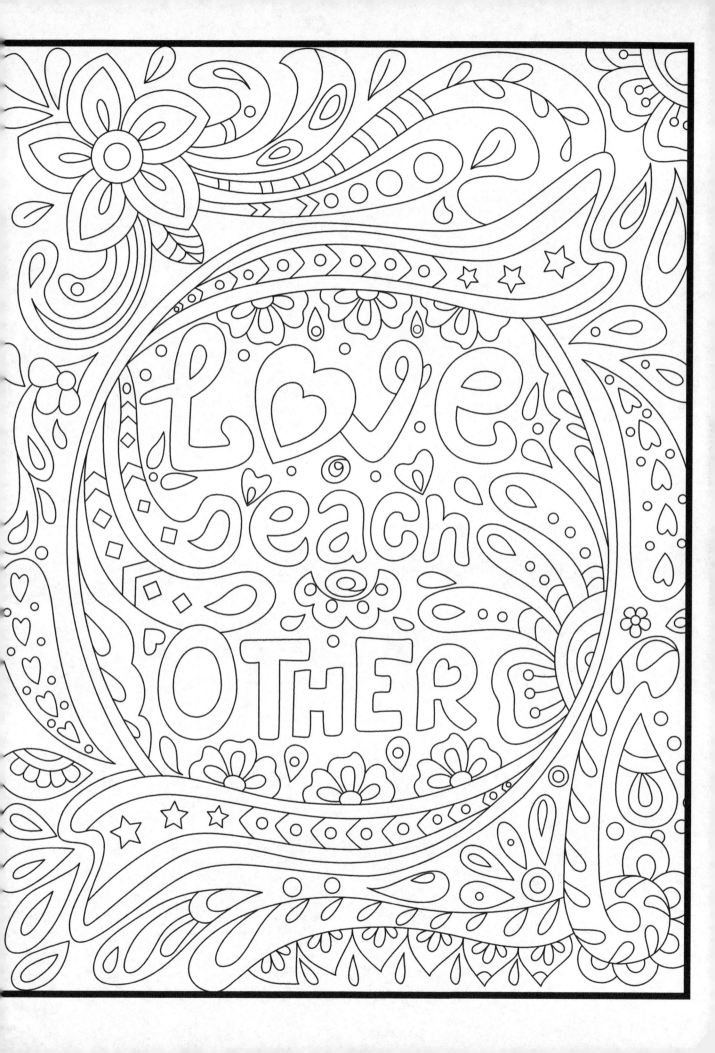

LEAVE MY AMAZON REVIEW

1. Go to Amazon
2. Search for *Jade Summer*
3. Find this book
4. Click the *Write a Review* button

JOIN US ON FACEBOOK

Facebook.com/JadeSummerColoring

Share your artwork, view artwork from other customers, and win free coloring books.

DOWNLOAD MY PDF VERSION

Go to **JadeSummer.com** and provide us with:

Title: **Inspirational Quotes**
Access Code: **43VZR747**

BUY DIGITAL VERSIONS ON ETSY

Etsy.com/shop/JadeSummerColoring

Download PDF versions of books, get individual coloring pages, and access exclusive discounts.

Made in the USA
Middletown, DE
11 April 2019